T0355028

Turn
your
PAIN
into
POWER

Turn *your* PAIN *into* POWER

Maya Coria

ARCHWAY
PUBLISHING

Archway Publishing books may be ordered through booksellers or by contacting:

Archway Publishing
1663 Liberty Drive
Bloomington, IN 47403
www.archwaypublishing.com
844-669-3957

ISBN: 978-1-6657-6700-2 (sc)
ISBN: 978-1-6657-6701-9 (e)

Library of Congress Control Number: 2024923082

Print information available on the last page.

Archway Publishing rev. date: 1/30/2025

Welcome

I am Maya Coria, the creator of this journal and your companion on your self-healing journey. This journal was created through my personal experiences and practices that helped me overcome numerous obstacles I've encountered over the years. The beginning of my hardest years started during COVID, I was pursing my nursing career and fell pregnant at the age of 20. Once I had my son at 21, I became a single mom battling postpartum depression and a few months later was kicked out of the nursing program due to sleep deprivation and juggling everything on my own. I felt like a failure to myself, my son and my family. I then got the idea to give myself a date to pour all of my emotions out in a journal for 2 weeks. Once those 2 weeks were over, I was no longer allowed to dwell on my situation but instead move forward with my head up high. I implemented these practices into my life and started seeing this drastic change on who I was becoming. Being able to experience my results I decided to share my techniques with my circle and also seen their results. This made me want to help as many people as possible since the outcomes of these practices have been working.

Over the course of nearly a month, you will engage in daily exercises and reflective practices designed to support your healing from trauma, heartbreak, or any emotional challenges you may be facing. With my guidance and support you will be taken on a challenging journey to bring forth the emotions and pain that have been deeply pushed and tucked away.

This journal was created for anyone and everyone. You don't have to be religious or spiritual to complete this journal. The bible is used as a tool to navigate through everyday life and not to push religion on anyone. Spirituality seeks a meaningful connection than something bigger than yourself. Everyone has their own story and beliefs and I invite you to show who you truly are in your very own self-healing journal. Step into your pain and turn it into power!

Turn Your Pain Into Power

Turning Your Pain into Power can be difficult, especially if
you're feeling alone. But remember, it's also one of the best gifts
you can give yourself—learning to value and love yourself.

Letting go of who you used to be creates room
for the most POWERFUL, ABUNDANT,
and STRONG MINDED person you
were always meant to be!

Understanding that self-healing from past traumas
will take some time but you are NOT alone!
You might face a lot of emotions and challenges along
the way, and this journal is here to be your safe space
to let it all out—your pain, stress, and anger.
This journal is just for you, a safe place where you can be
honest with yourself and really dive into your healing.

You are WORTHY, LOVED, POWERFUL,
ABUNDANT and STRONG MINDED!
Now this is your time to finally see it as well.

Lets get to work!

Contents

Guideline Part 2

Guideline Part 1

This journal is here to help you heal from past traumas and let go of old versions of yourself. Whether you are going through a breakup, loss, or just have to heal your mental health, this journal provides a structured tool for your journey.

Upon completing your healing journal, you have the option to either keep or dispose this journal.

How Does This Work?

Step 1: Put your intentions towards your journal.
   -Cleanse, pray, meditate with journal

Step 2: Pick a <u>realistic</u> time frame for your heart/mind/body that will need to heal and move forward from your trauma.
   -Six days, two weeks, a month
   Example 1: A breakup: 2 weeks to cry, be angry, feel every emotion towards that person but no longer than 2 weeks.
   Example 2: A loss due to death: A month to let out every emotion towards this heartbreak but no more than a month.

Step 3: Sign "<u>I Promise</u>" page
   -Signing the I Promise page is a contract to yourself to stick with the time frame of your choice and complete the entire journal.

Reminder: This is your healing journey and only you can make this promise to reach the upmost healed version of yourself.

Step 4: Recite your commitments each day

Step 5: Complete Personal Reflection Page

-Helping you stay on top of your goals for your healing journey.

Step 6: Journal every day for the amount of time you agreed to in your self-contract on the "I Promise" page.

I Promise

This is your personal self healing commitment contract. This contract is designed to be a powerful tool in your self-healing journey, serving as both a reminder of your commitment and a source of empowerment as you continue to grow and transform.

I _____ make this solemn promise to myself,
      First   Last

committing fully to my journey of self-healing, growth, and transformation. I recognize that this path may be challenging, but I am dedicated to following it through with courage, perseverance, and self-love.

I will start my healing journey on _____ and will complete the
                                           Date
first chapter by _____.
               Date

I promise myself to commit to the dates above to complete the first chapter of my healing journal. I promise to allow myself to express my emotions and to heal from my past trauma(s). Once I have completed the first chapter in my journal I promise to not go back and dwell on my past. I promise to move forward and complete the rest of the journal with a clean open heart and mindset.

By signing below, I enter into this binding contract with myself. I understand that this commitment is an act of self-love, and I vow to follow through with determination and kindness, honoring the promises I have made.

Signature: _____

Date: _____

Commitments

1. I promise to honor my needs.
   - I will take the time to listen to my inner voice and prioritize my mental, emotional, and physical well-being. I commit to nourishing my mind, body, and soul with love and care.

2. I promise to face my fears.
   - I will not run from the things that scare me. Instead, I will confront them with bravery, knowing that through facing my fears, I will find growth and freedom.

3. I promise to forgive myself and others.
   - I will let go of past grievances and extend forgiveness, understanding that it is essential for my peace and healing.

4. I promise to embrace my imperfections.
   - I will acknowledge my flaws without judgment and treat myself with compassion. I know that these imperfections make me human and contribute to my unique beauty.

5. I promise to set boundaries.
   - I will protect my energy by setting healthy boundaries, saying "no" when necessary, and surrounding myself with people who uplift and support my journey.

6. I promise to be patient with my progress.
   - I will celebrate every step forward, no matter how small, and remind myself that healing is not linear. I will give myself grace in moments of struggle.

7. I promise to stay committed.
   - I will not give up on myself, even when the road gets tough. I am worthy of the effort, time, and love it takes to heal and grow.

· · · · · ·●))) ● (((· · · · · ·

Personal Reflection

In this journey, I specifically commit to:

Healing from:

_____

_____

_____

Growing into:

_____

_____

_____

Letting go of:

_____

_____

_____

Embracing:

_____

_____

_____

· · · · •••))) ● (((•••• · · ·

Chapter 1

You have now entered the first chapter in your healing journey. As you move through this initial chapter, you may experience a range of emotions. It is important to remember this journal is a sacred space, created solely for you to explore and express your inner world. While completing all 14 days is not mandatory, you have the flexibility to extend your journaling as needed to fully process your emotions. Acknowledge and appreciate the significant step you've taken toward healing and personal growth.

Now let's get to work!

Date: _____

Day 1

Day 2

Date: _____

Day 3

Date: _____

Day 4

Reminder

Whenever you feel overwhelmed, try to pause and take a few deep breaths. It's a simple way to help calm your mind and body.

This breathing technique helps anxiety, panic attacks, overthinking, insomnia, lowering stress levels, grounding etc.

Breathing technique: 6-3-6-3 (5x)
Inhale for 6 counts, hold for 3, exhale for 6
counts hold for 3 - repeat 5-7 times

Date: _____

Day 5

_____

_____

_____

_____

_____

_____

_____

_____

_____

_____

_____

_____

_____

_____

_____

_____

_____

Day 6

Day 7

Day 8

_____

_____

_____

_____

_____

_____

_____

_____

_____

_____

_____

_____

_____

_____

_____

_____

_____

_____

_____

_____

Reminder

It's okay to have days when you don't feel like moving
forward. Just remember that even on the hardest days,
you are making progress by simply continuing.

It's important to prioritize your well-being during this time.
You might feel some hesitation about focusing on yourself, but
please know that self-care is not selfish, it's a vital part of healing.
While journaling your emotions can be challenging, it can also
be a profoundly beneficial practice for your healing journey.

Self-Care Practices:
Journal
Working out
Read a book
Meditate/ Pray
Take a walk outside
Make sleep a priority
Seek professional support
etc.

Day 10

· · · · ·•••))) ● (((•••••· ·

Date: _____

Day 11

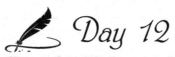

Date: _____

Day 12

Reminder

Every step you've taken has brought you closer to where you want to be. You're so close to reaching the end of this particular chapter of your self healing journey. Remember to stay gentle with yourself you're almost there!

Reflect on your commitments:

- I promise to honor my needs.
- I promise to face my fears.
- I promise to forgive myself and others.
- I will take the time to listen to my inner voice and prioritize my mental, emotional, and physical well-being. I commit to nourishing my mind, body, and soul with love and care.
- I will not run from the things that scare me. Instead, I will confront them with bravery, knowing that through facing my fears, I will find growth and freedom.
- I promise to embrace my imperfections.
- I will let go of past grievances and extend forgiveness, understanding that it is essential for my peace and healing.

Day 13

_____

_____

_____

_____

_____

_____

_____

_____

_____

_____

_____

_____

_____

_____

_____

Day 14

_____

_____

_____

_____

_____

_____

_____

_____

_____

_____

_____

_____

_____

_____

_____

_____

_____

_____

_____

_____

_____

Guideline Part 2

Congratulations on completing chapter 1 of your healing journal!

Leaving the pain and trauma in chapter 1 we are now moving on to the excitement and joy of chapter 2.

Chapter 2 will be your journey of self healing, self exploration, goal setting, accomplishments, reflection and so much more!

How chapter 2 works

Every morning:

Mood tracker: Tracking your mood/ emotion will help you acknowledge your well-being for the day.

Set Goals: Setting goals will help you stay consistent and focus on the positive growth you are willing to achieve.

Schedule: Writing down your schedule will help you stay organized, improve time management, increase productivity, reduce stress, and achieve goals.

Every evening:

Reflect: By taking time to reflect on your day, you can gain valuable insights, gain personal development, and improve overall well-being.

Question of the Day: Each day will have a different question for you to answer. This will help you become aware of the inner work that still needs to be worked upon.

Meditation/ Prayer Notes: Taking note of any messages received by meditation or prayer helps you stay in tune and supports your well being with both spiritual and psychological growth.

Check List: Completing a check list throughout the day helps you stay accountable for your spiritual and physical growth.

Chapter 2

You have now entered the second chapter in your healing journey. In this chapter, you'll be diving into some deep inner work over the next 10 days. Chapter 2 is here to help you stay centered and keep moving forward with your tasks, while continuing to grow into the healed version of yourself.

It's all about exploring the inner work that's essential
for your healing journey. Helping you connect to
your body, mind and spirit and guiding you to truly
understand and embrace your inner wisdom.

Forgiveness

fr·giv·nuhs

Definition:

> Forgiveness is a conscious, deliberate decision to
> release feelings of resentment or vengeance toward
> a person or group who has harmed you.

Forgiveness gently restores the forgiver's peace of mind and liberates them from the burden of lingering anger. It is the intentional act of letting go of resentment, anger, or the desire for retribution toward someone who has caused harm or wrongdoing. It involves releasing negative emotions and choosing to move forward without holding a grudge. Forgiveness does not necessarily mean forgetting or excusing the offense, but rather, it is about finding inner peace and freeing oneself from the ongoing emotional impact of the hurt.

Benefits of Forgiveness:
Emotional Relief
Reduced Stress
Improved Mental Health
Better Relationships
Enhanced Physical Health
Personal Growth
Increased Compassion
Freedom from the Past
Strengthen Resilience

How am I feeling today?

○ ○ ○ ○ ○

Very Sad ←→ Truly Happy

Forgiveness

Today's Goals & Intentions:

My agenda for today:

Have I forgiven others
who've hurt me?

Affirmations:
I forgive myself for my mistakes.
I am ready to let go of what no longer serves me.
I am embracing myself just as I am.

Reminders:
My past does not define who I am today.
Do not allow a bad moment turn into a bad day.
Everything always happens for a reason and it will
always benefit me one way or another.

Bible verse of the day:
Ephesians 4:32
"Be kind and compassionate to one another,
forgive each other, as God in Christ forgave you."

Today's Reflection:

How am I feeling tonight?

○ ○ ○ ○ ○

Very Sad ←→ Truly Happy

What is holding me back from
fully forgiving myself?

Is there anything I could've
done better today?

How can I make tomorrow better than today?

Meditation/ Prayer notes:

Check List

☐ Drink at least 6 cups of water

☐ Eat at least 2 meals

☐ Light Exercise & Stretch

☐ Spend at least 10 minutes outside/ Grounding

☐ Journal

☐ Prepare for tomorrow

☐ Meditate/ Pray

Healing

hee·luhng

Definition:

The process of restoring health, well-being, or balance, whether it be physical, emotional, mental, or spiritual. It involves the recovery and repair of an individual's body, mind, or spirit from illness, injury, trauma, or distress.

From a spiritual perspective, healing can be seen as a journey towards self-awareness and inner peace. It involves understanding and addressing emotional, mental, and spiritual blocks that may be contributing to one's suffering. This process often includes forgiveness, self-compassion, and the release of past traumas or negative patterns. Many spiritual traditions view healing as a way to reconnect with a higher self or divine essence. In this sense, healing is about realigning with one's true nature and purpose. It might involve practices like meditation, prayer, or energy work to facilitate this connection and foster a sense of unity with the larger whole.

Benefits of Healing:
Physical Health Improvement
Emotional Resilience
Mental Clarity
Enhanced Relationships
Increased Self-Awareness
Greater Inner Peace
Strengthened Spiritual Connection
Personal Growth
Increased Vitality and Joy
Improved Quality of Life

How am I feeling today?

○ ○ ○ ○ ○

Very Sad ⟷ Truly Happy

Healing

Date: _____

Today's Goals & Intentions:

My agenda for today:

Things I am grateful for:

Affirmations:

I give myself permission to heal
I accept the lesson my pain is offering me
I know these circumstances are a gift to help me grow.

Reminders:

While I heal, it is okay for me to take time for myself.
Healing is a process, be patient and gentle with yourself .
Healing myself will help heal others.

Bible verse of the day:

Jeremiah 33:6
"Nevertheless, I will bring health and healing to it; I will heal my
people and will let them enjoy abundant peace and security."

Today's Reflection:

_____

_____

_____

_____

_____

_____

_____

_____

_____

_____

_____

_____

_____

How am I feeling tonight?

○ ○ ○ ○ ○

Very Sad ⟷ Truly Happy

How are my thoughts lately?
Are they serving me or
holding me back?

Is there anything I could've
done better today?

How can I make tomorrow better than today?

Meditation/ Prayer notes:

Check List

☐ Drink at least 6 cups of water

☐ Eat at least 2 meals

☐ Light Exercise & Stretch

☐ Spend at least 10 minutes outside/ Grounding

☐ Journal

☐ Prepare for tomorrow

☐ Meditate/ Pray

Self-love

self ˈlʌv

Definition:

Self-love is the practice of caring for and valuing oneself with kindness, compassion, and respect.

It involves recognizing your own worth and treating yourself with the same empathy and consideration you would offer to a loved one. Here are some key aspects of self-love: Self- Acceptance, Self-Compassion, Healthy Boundaries, Self-Care, Positive Self-Talk, Personal Growth, Forgiveness, and Gratitude for Self.

Benefits of Self-love:
Improved Mental Health
Increased Self-Esteem
Better Emotional Regulation
Healthier Relationships
Enhanced Resilience
Increased Self-Awareness
Greater Life Satisfaction
Better Physical Health
Personal Growth
Authenticity
Inner Peace

How am I feeling today?

○ ○ ○ ○ ○

Very Sad ⟷ Truly Happy

Self-love

Date: _____

Today's Goals & Intentions:

My agenda for today:

Things I love about myself:

Affirmations:

I Am Enough
I Am Powerful
I Love Myself

I allow my heart to heal
I am worth enough to be
loved unconditionally

Reminders:

I am someone's dream person.
I forgive myself for not putting myself first.
My inner child is waiting to be loved by this new version of myself.

Bible verse of the day:

1 Corinthians 13:4-8
"Love is patient, love is kind. It does not envy, it does not boast, it is not proud.

It does not dishonor others, it is not self-seeking, it is
not easily angered, it keeps no record of wrongs.
Love does not delight in evil but rejoices with the truth.
It always protects, always trusts, always hopes, always perseveres.
Love never fails."

Today's Reflection:

_____

_____

_____

_____

_____

_____

_____

_____

_____

_____

_____

_____

_____

_____

How am I feeling tonight?

○ ○ ○ ○ ○

Very Sad ⟷ Truly Happy

Things I need to work on
to love myself more:

Is there anything I could've
done better today?

How can I make tomorrow better than today?

Meditation/ Prayer notes:

Check List

☐ Drink at least 6 cups of water

☐ Eat at least 2 meals

☐ Light Exercise & Stretch

☐ Spend at least 10 minutes outside/ Grounding

☐ Journal

☐ Prepare for tomorrow

☐ Meditate/ Pray

Emotional Well-Being

eh-MOH-shun-uhl · wel-BEE-ing

Definition:

Emotional well-being refers to the state of having a positive, balanced, and healthy emotional state. It involves the ability to manage and express emotions effectively, maintain a sense of satisfaction and fulfillment, and cope with life's challenges in a constructive way.

Spiritual emotional well-being is about cultivating a deep sense of peace, connection, and purpose through alignment with your inner self and spiritual beliefs. It integrates emotional health with spiritual practices, fostering a holistic and fulfilling life

Benefits of Emotional well-being:
Enhanced Mental Health
Improved Physical Health
Better Relationships
Increased Resilience
Greater Life Satisfaction
Enhanced Self-Esteem
Better Coping Skills
Increased Creativity
and Productivity
Overall Quality of
Life Healthy Habits

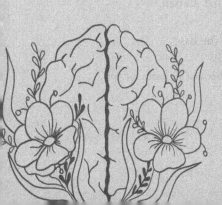

How am I feeling today?

○ ○ ○ ○ ○

Very Sad ⟷ Truly Happy

Emotional Well-Being

Date: _____

Today's Goals & Intentions:

My agenda for today:

What emotion(s) am I
feeling right now?

Affirmations:
I let go of negative self-talk.
How I feel matters.
I am in control of my emotions.

Reminders:
Every emotion is temporary.
Self care is not selfish.
Take time away to embrace how you feel.
Make time to ground yourself.

Bible verse of the day:
1 Peter 5:7
"Cast all your anxiety on him because he cares for you."

Today's Reflection:

_____

_____

_____

_____

_____

_____

_____

_____

_____

_____

_____

_____

_____

_____

_____

· · · · • • •)) 🌑 ● (((• • • • • ·

How am I feeling tonight?

○ ○ ○ ○ ○

Very Sad ←→ Truly Happy

What are some things I am stressing about that are out of my control?

Is there anything I could've done better today?

How can I make tomorrow better than today?

Meditation/ Prayer notes:

Check List

☐ Drink at least 6 cups of water

☐ Eat at least 2 meals

☐ Light Exercise & Stretch

☐ Spend at least 10 minutes outside/ Grounding

☐ Journal

☐ Prepare for tomorrow

☐ Meditate/ Pray

Inner Peace

IN-ur · PEES

Definition:

A state of mental and emotional calm and contentment that comes from within oneself.

In a spiritual aspect, Inner peace is a profound state of tranquility that arises from a deep connection to the divine, alignment with your higher self, and acceptance of life's flow. It transcends external circumstances and reflects a deep sense of harmony and unity with God / the universe. Some key elements to understand inner peace are: Mental Calmness, Emotional Stability, Acceptance and Surrender, Harmony, Connection to Values, Purpose and Meaning.

Benefits of Inner Peace:

Emotional Stability

Improved Mental Clarity

Enhanced Resilience

Increased Self-Awareness

Improved Relationships

Greater Life Satisfaction

Enhanced Creativity and Productivity

Reduced Conflict

Increased Compassion

Alignment with Values

Enhanced Spiritual Connection

How am I feeling today?

○ ○ ○ ○ ○

Very Sad ⟷ Truly Happy

Inner Peace

Date: _____

Today's Goals & Intentions:

My agenda for today:

Things that are blocking
my inner peace:

Affirmations:

I choose to embrace peace and tranquility.
I inhale peace and exhale worry.
I trust the process and am becoming who I am meant to be.

Reminders:

Take a deep breath...release
You are not what happened to you. Do not allow others or
an event control your thoughts. You are what you become in
this very moment. By letting go, you can begin again.

Bible verse of the day:

2 Thessalonians 3:16
"Now may the Lord of peace himself give you peace at all
times in every way. The Lord be with all of you."

Today's Reflection:

_____

_____

_____

_____

_____

_____

_____

_____

_____

_____

_____

_____

_____

_____

How am I feeling tonight?

○ ○ ○ ○ ○

Very Sad ⟷ Truly Happy

What are things I can start
doing to find inner peace?

Is there anything I could've
done better today?

How can I make tomorrow better than today?

Meditation/ Prayer notes:

Check List

☐ Drink at least 6 cups of water

☐ Eat at least 2 meals

☐ Light Exercise & Stretch

☐ Spend at least 10 minutes outside/ Grounding

☐ Journal

☐ Prepare for tomorrow

☐ Meditate/ Pray

Gratitude

GRAT-i-tood

Definition:

The feeling or expression of thankfulness and appreciation for something received, whether it is a tangible gift, an act of kindness, or a positive experience. It involves recognizing and valuing the good things in life and acknowledging the contributions of others.

These are many different ways to show gratitude. Here are a few examples:

- Express gratitude: Writing a thank-you note, sending a text, or saying "thank you" verbally.
- Keep a gratitude journal: Write down the things you are grateful for each day.
- Practice gratitude meditation: Reflect on things you are thankful for to connect with a deeper sense of appreciation.
- Perform acts of kindness: Show appreciation for the people who make your life better by doing favors, complimenting them, or reaching out to them.
- Appreciate everything: Show appreciation for people for everything they do.
- Volunteer in your community. Write a list of things that bring you joy. Send a thank you gift.
- Take someone out for a meal.
- Return a favor

Benefits of Gratitude:

Improved Mental Health
Increased Happiness
Better Relationships
Boosted Self-Esteem
Improved Physical Health
Enhanced Empathy and Compassion
Better Sleep
Increased Mindfulness
Strengthened Immune System
Reduced Stress

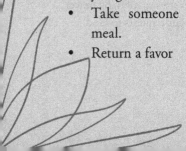

How am I feeling today?

○ ○ ○ ○ ○

Very Sad ⟷ Truly Happy

Gratitude

Date: _____

Today's Goals & Intentions:

My agenda for today:

How often do I give myself thanks?

Affirmations:
I am thankful for the strength and resilience within me.
Life is a gift, and I am grateful for every moment.

Reminders:
Embracing lessons and fresh starts allows you to heal quicker.
Growth comes with pain. You are so much stronger than you may see.
Allow yourself to say thank you for overcoming
every obstacal that came your way.

Bible verse of the day:
Philippians 4:6
"Do not be anxious about anything, but in every situation, by prayer
and petition, with thanksgiving, present your requests to God."

Today's Reflection:

_____

_____

_____

_____

_____

_____

_____

_____

_____

_____

_____

_____

_____

_____

_____

_____

How am I feeling tonight?

○ ○ ○ ○ ○

Very Sad ⟷ Truly Happy

What am I thankful for?

Is there anything I could've done better today?

How can I make tomorrow better than today?

Meditation/ Prayer notes:

Check List

☐   Drink at least 6 cups of water

☐   Eat at least 2 meals

☐   Light Exercise & Stretch

☐   Spend at least 10 minutes outside/ Grounding

☐   Journal

☐   Prepare for tomorrow

☐   Meditate/ Pray

Courage & Strength

KUR-ij · STR-engk-th

Definition:

Courage is the ability to confront fear, pain, danger, or adversity with bravery and resolve. It involves acting in the face of challenges despite feeling afraid or uncertain. Courage can manifest in various ways, from physical acts of bravery to moral and emotional fortitude.

Strength is the quality or state of being physically, mentally, or emotionally resilient. It refers to the capacity to endure, withstand, or overcome challenges and adversities, whether they are physical, mental, or emotional in nature.

While courage and strength are distinct qualities, they often complement each other. Courage is about taking action despite fear, and strength involves the endurance and resilience to face and overcome challenges.

Benefits of Courage & Strength:
Overcoming Fears
Achieving Goals
Building Confidence
Enhanced Mental Toughness
Emotional Stability
Effective Problem Solving
Holistic Well-being
Leadership and Influence
Endurance and Resilience
Improved Health

How am I feeling today?

○ ○ ○ ○ ○

Very Sad ←→ Truly Happy

Courage & Strength

Date: _____

Today's Goals & Intentions:

My agenda for today:

Strengths I have:

Affirmations:
I am strong and courageous.
My courage gives others strength.
With my strength and courage I am able to
conquer any obstacle life brings me.

Reminders:
TURN YOUR PAIN INTO POWER
Courage is resistance and mastery of fear.
Hold your head up high, look fear in the face and
show your strength, courage and confidence.

Bible verse of the day:
Deuteronomy 31:6
"Be strong and courageous. Do not be afraid or terrified
because of them, for the Lord your God goes with
you; he will never leave you nor forsake you."

Today's Reflection:

_____

_____

_____

_____

_____

_____

_____

_____

_____

_____

_____

_____

_____

_____

_____

How am I feeling tonight?

○ ○ ○ ○ ○

Very Sad ←→ Truly Happy

What do I need to work on
to strengthen my mindset?

Is there anything I could've
done better today?

How can I make tomorrow better than today?

Meditation/ Prayer notes:

Check List

☐ Drink at least 6 cups of water

☐ Eat at least 2 meals

☐ Light Exercise & Stretch

☐ Spend at least 10 minutes outside/ Grounding

☐ Journal

☐ Prepare for tomorrow

☐ Meditate/ Pray

Boundaries

BOUND-reez

Definition:

Boundaries are essentially limits or edges that delineate different areas, whether they are physical, emotional, social, or conceptual. They serve to define, protect, and manage the interactions between different entities, ensuring clarity and respect.

Physical Boundaries
Personal Boundaries
Professional Boundaries
Conceptual Boundaries

Spiritual boundaries help you navigate your spiritual journey in a way that maintains your integrity, well-being, and personal growth. They allow you to engage with your spiritual practices and community in a manner that supports and honors your individual spiritual path while respecting the boundaries of others.

Personal Spiritual Space
Respecting Beliefs
Protecting Your Energy
Balancing Spiritual and
Everyday Life

Benefits of Boundaries:
Improved Self-Care
Healthier Relationships
Enhanced Emotional Health
Increased Productivity and Focus
Greater Self-Awareness
Enhanced Communication Skills
Better Work-Life Balance
Increased Confidence and Empowerment
Enhanced Personal and
Professional Relationships
Reduction in Resentment and Burnout

115

How am I feeling today?

◯ ◯ ◯ ◯ ◯

Very Sad ⟷ Truly Happy

Boundaries

Date: _____

Today's Goals & Intentions:

My agenda for today:

Have I set new boundaries
since my trauma?

Affirmations:
My time and energy are valuable
It's okay to say **NO**
I deserve to put myself **FIRST**

Reminders:
It is healthy and necessary to put boundaries.
Setting boundaries allows you to stay true to yourself.
It is okay to say no to things and people who do not align with your values.

Bible verse of the day:
Matthew 5:37
"All you need to say is simply 'Yes' or 'No'; anything
beyond this comes from the evil one."

Today's Reflection:

_____

_____

_____

_____

_____

_____

_____

_____

_____

_____

_____

_____

_____

_____

_____

_____

· · ·· ···))) ● (((· ···· · ·

How am I feeling tonight?

○ ○ ○ ○ ○

Very Sad ←→ Truly Happy

What new boundaries do I need to set to improve my overall health?

Is there anything I could've done better today?

How can I make tomorrow better than today?

Meditation/ Prayer notes:

Check List

☐ Drink at least 6 cups of water

☐ Eat at least 2 meals

☐ Light Exercise & Stretch

☐ Spend at least 10 minutes outside/ Grounding

☐ Journal

☐ Prepare for tomorrow

☐ Meditate/ Pray

I AM

eye'm

Definition:

In a spiritual sense, "I AM" encapsulates the essence of existence, the divine nature of being, and the profound awareness of one's self in the grand scheme of life and the universe.

- Divine Presence: In many spiritual traditions, "I AM" is associated with the divine or God. For example, in the Bible, God identifies Himself to Moses as "I AM WHO I AM" (Exodus 3:14), which signifies the eternal, self- sustaining nature of the divine.
- Self-Awareness: In existential and spiritual philosophies, "I AM" represents self-awareness and the fundamental experience of one's own existence. It's a declaration of being and consciousness, emphasizing the awareness of one's own presence and identity.
- Unity with the Divine: Some spiritual teachings, particularly in Eastern philosophies like Advaita Vedanta, view "I AM" as a recognition of the self's unity with the universal consciousness or Brahman. It underscores the idea that the individual self (Atman) is fundamentally one with the greater divine reality.
- Present Moment: "I AM" can also signify living in the present moment. It's about experiencing and acknowledging your existence here and now, free from past or future distractions.

- Affirmation of Being: In some New Age or personal growth practices, "I AM" is used in affirmations to reinforce a positive sense of self and personal empowerment, such as "I am confident" or "I am at peace."

Benefits of I AM:

Boosts Self-Esteem and Confidence
Promotes Goal Achievement
Enhances Mental Well-Being
Encourages a Growth Mindset
Strengthens Positive Habits
Improves Relationships
Supports Manifestation

How am I feeling today?

○ ○ ○ ○ ○
Very Sad ←→ Truly Happy

I AM

Date: _____

Today's Goals & Intentions:

My agenda for today:

Do I usually speak positive or negative about myself? Why?

Affirmations:

I AM worthy
I AM loved
I AM successful

I AM financially free
I AM the master of my wealth

Reminders:
Repeating I AM affirmations helps reprogram your subconscious mind and replace negative self-talk with empowering beliefs.
I AM is very powerful, so be aware of how you speak about yourself.

Bible verse of the day:
1 Corinthians 15:10
"But by the grace of God I am what I am, and his grace to me was not without effect. No, I worked harder than all of them, yet not I, but the grace of God that is with me."

Today's Reflection:

_____

_____

_____

_____

_____

_____

_____

_____

_____

_____

_____

_____

_____

_____

_____

_____

How am I feeling tonight?

○ ○ ○ ○ ○

Very Sad ←→ Truly Happy

List 5 "I AM" Affirmations
I'll start using daily:

Is there anything I could've
done better today?

How can I make tomorrow better than today?

Meditation/ Prayer notes:

Check List

☐ Drink at least 6 cups of water

☐ Eat at least 2 meals

☐ Light Exercise & Stretch

☐ Spend at least 10 minutes outside/ Grounding

☐ Journal

☐ Prepare for tomorrow

☐ Meditate/ Pray

How to manifest properly

Manifesting effectively involves focusing your thoughts, emotions, and actions to attract what you want into your life. Manifestation is about aligning your thoughts, emotions, and actions with your desires, while staying open to possibilities and trusting the process.

Here's a guide on how to manifest properly:

1. Clarify Your Desire
   - Be specific about what you want. The clearer your intention, the more focused your energy will be. Write it down or visualize it in detail.

2. Believe in Your Desire
   - Truly believe that what you desire is possible and that you deserve it. This helps align your energy with your goal.

3. Visualize with Emotion
   - Regularly imagine yourself already having what you want. Engage all your senses in this visualization. Feel the emotions that come with achieving your desire (joy, peace, satisfaction).

4. Affirmations
   - Use positive affirmations to reinforce your belief in your desire. Frame them in the present tense as though your desire is already a reality ("I am attracting abundance into my life").

5. Let Go of Doubt
   - Release limiting beliefs or doubts that may block your manifestation. Challenge negative thoughts and replace them with affirmations of possibility and faith.

6. Take Aligned Action
   - Manifesting isn't just about thinking positively; it requires taking steps toward your goal. Look for opportunities, act on inspiration, and take practical actions to bring your desire closer.

7. Gratitude
   - Express gratitude for what you already have and for what you are manifesting. Gratitude raises your vibration and aligns you with more positive outcomes.

8. Let Go and Trust
   - Once you've set your intention and taken action, release attachment to the outcome. Trust that God, the universe (or whatever higher power you believe in) will bring it to you at the right time.

9. Stay Positive and Patient
   - Stay open, positive, and patient. Manifestation may not happen overnight, but keep faith that it's on its way.

Manifesting

man-i-fes-TAY-shun

Definition:

The process of making something clear, evident, or real, whether it's through deliberate intention, psychological expression, or simply observable outcomes.

Spiritually manifestation often refers to the practice of focusing thoughts, desires, or intentions to attract or create specific outcomes in one's life. This is based on the idea that positive thinking and visualization can bring about desired results.

Psychologically manifestation can also refer to the observable expression of internal thoughts, feelings, or psychological states. For instance, someone might manifest their anxiety through physical symptoms or behavioral changes.

Benefits of Manifestation:
Clarity and Focus
Increased Motivation
Positive Mindset
Enhanced Creativity and Problem-Solving
Improved Emotional Well-Being
Better Decision-Making
Strengthened Resilience
Manifestation of Opportunities
Personal Growth

How am I feeling today?

○ ○ ○ ○ ○

Very Sad ⟷ Truly Happy

Manifesting

Date: _____

Today's Goals & Intentions:

My agenda for today:

Ways I manifest:

Affirmations:

I am grateful for another day to manifest my dreams.

I am open to receiving abundance in all areas of my life.

Reminders:

Its up to you to change your life. No one can do it for you.

Your dream life is possible!

It won't be easy but how badly do you want it?

Bible verse of the day:

Matthew 6:33

"But seek first his kingdom and his righteousness, and
all these things will be given to you as well."

Today's Reflection:

How am I feeling tonight?

○ ○ ○ ○ ○

Very Sad ⟷ Truly Happy

What are somethings I
want to manifest?

Is there anything I could've
done better today?

How can I make tomorrow better than today?

Meditation/ Prayer notes:

Check List

☐ Drink at least 6 cups of water

☐ Eat at least 2 meals

☐ Light Exercise & Stretch

☐ Spend at least 10 minutes outside/ Grounding

☐ Journal

☐ Prepare for tomorrow

☐ Meditate/ Pray

My Successes

Write down all your successes you've accomplished.

How to Meditate and Visualize Spiritually Before Manifesting and Journaling to Your Future Self

Meditation and visualization are powerful practices that can enhance your ability to manifest your goals and connect with your future self. Here's a step-by-step guide to help you through the process.

Step 1: Create a Calm Space
- Find a quiet and comfortable space where you won't be disturbed. This could be a cozy corner of your home, a serene spot in nature, or anywhere you feel at peace. Dim the lights, light a candle, or play soft music if it helps set the mood.

Step 2: Get Comfortable
- Sit or lie down in a comfortable position. You can sit cross-legged on the floor, in a chair with your feet flat on the ground, or even lie down. Close your eyes gently and take a few deep breaths to center yourself.

Step 3: Focus on Your Breath
- Begin by focusing on your breath. Inhale deeply through your nose, allowing your abdomen to rise, and exhale slowly through your mouth. Repeat this for several minutes, letting your breath become steady and natural. This practice helps quiet your mind and brings your awareness into the present moment. You can also reflect on 6-3-6-3 exercise in part 1.

Step 4: Set Your Intention
- Once you feel relaxed, set a clear intention for your meditation. This could be something like, "I am open to receiving guidance from my future self," or "I seek clarity on my goals." Speak this intention silently to yourself or write it down before you start.

Step 5: Visualize Your Future Self
- With your intention in mind, begin to visualize your future self. Imagine yourself in a few months or years, living the life you desire. Picture the details—what you're doing, where you are, how you feel. Engage all your senses: see the colors around you, hear the sounds, feel the emotions of joy and fulfillment.

Step 6: Connect Spiritually
- As you visualize, take a moment to connect spiritually. You can imagine a warm light surrounding you, representing love and support from the universe. Feel this energy as you envision your future self. Allow yourself to receive any insights or messages that come to you during this time.

Step 7: Embrace Gratitude
- As you conclude your visualization, embrace a sense of gratitude. Thank your future self for the guidance and inspiration. Feel grateful for the journey ahead and the positive changes you're working toward.

Step 8: Transition to Journaling
- When you feel ready, gently bring your awareness back to the present. Open your eyes and take a few deep breaths. Now, it's time to journal. Write about your experience in meditation, the feelings that arose, and any insights you

gained about your future self. You can also jot down specific goals or steps you want to take toward manifesting your desires.

Step 9: Manifest
* Finally, use the energy and clarity gained from your meditation and journaling to manifest your goals. Visualize them as already achieved and take inspired actions that align with your intentions. Trust in the process and remain open to the opportunities that come your way.

By incorporating meditation and visualization into your practice, you can deepen your connection to your future self and enhance your ability to manifest the life you desire. Remember, this is a journey, so be patient and compassionate with yourself as you grow.

A Letter to Your Future Self

In this exercise, you will first start with meditation
and visualization to your future self.
One you've entered this state of mind you will then write
a heartfelt letter to your future self, celebrating all the
accomplishments and achievements you will have attained
over the next year. This future letter serves as a powerful
tool for self-reflection once the year comes to a close.

Take a moment to write down everything you've
overcome, transformed, and achieved.
Dive deep into your imagination, visualize your dreams and
describe the feelings, emotions, colors, and sense of worth
that come with your success. Allow yourself to step into the
experience of living your ideal life as if it were happening today.

Remember, you are worthy of abundance and capable
of creating the life of your dreams. When an idea pops
in your mind, it's a sign that it's meant for you. This is
your chance to turn the impossible, possible. Believe in
yourself and transition your dream into your reality.

Read this letter every night before bed to reinforce
your vision and invite your dreams to unfold.

Congratulations

Congratulations on completing the two-part healing journal!
This achievement is a testament to your incredible consistency,
self-love, motivation, and dedication throughout your journey
of self-healing. Taking the initial step toward healing can be
incredibly challenging, yet you embraced it with true courage.
You've journeyed through some of the deepest parts of your
healing, confronting your most challenging traumas head-on.
This important part of your spiritual journey has allowed
you to move past old wounds and transform into a more
empowered version of yourself. Your progress brings you closer
to embodying the person you have always aspired to be.
Take a moment to celebrate this amazing accomplishment and
recognize the immense growth you have achieved. You have truly
embraced your path to healing, and the future holds endless
possibilities as you continue to evolve. Congratulations on reaching
this significant milestone— you have done exceptionally well!

You've reached this significant milestone, and now have
the opportunity to either continue free writing about the
rest of your journey or close this chapter and focus on
achieving your new goals. You may choose to keep or discard
the journal, depending on what feels right for you.
I want to honor you for this special transition in your
life and for placing your trust in this process to support
your healing journey. Sending you lots of love and
strength as you enter this next phase of your life.
May you always be guided and blessed on your path.

-Maya

Affirmations

Forgiveness:

I forgive myself for my mistakes.
I am ready to let go of what no longer serves me.
I am embracing myself just as I am.

Healing:

I give myself permission to heal
I accept the lesson my pain is offering me
I know these circumstances are a gift to help me grow.

Self- Love:

I am someone's dream person.
I forgive myself for not putting myself first.
My inner child is waiting to be loved by this new version of myself.

Emotional Well-Being:

I let go of negative self-talk.
How I feel matters.
I am in control of my emotions.

Inner Peace:

I choose to embrace peace and tranquility.
I inhale peace and exhale worry.
I trust the process and am becoming who I am meant to be.

Gratitude:

I am thankful for the strength and resilience within me.
Life is a gift, and I am grateful for every moment.

Courage & Strength:

I am strong and courageous.
My courage gives others strength.
With my strength and courage I am able to
conquer any obstacle life brings me.

Boundaries:

My time and energy are valuable
It's okay to say NO
I deserve to put myself FIRST

I AM:

I AM worthy   I AM financially free
I AM loved   I AM the master of my wealth
I AM successful

Manifesting:

I am grateful for another day to manifest my dreams.
I am open to receiving abundance in all areas of my life.

· · · · ••))) ● (((•• · · · ·

Bible Verses

Forgiveness:

Ephesians 4:32
"Be kind and compassionate to one another, forgive
each other, as God in Christ forgave you."

Healing:

Jeremiah 33:6
"Nevertheless, I will bring health and healing to it; I will heal my
people and will let them enjoy abundant peace and security."

Self- Love:

1 Corinthians 13:4-8
"Love is patient, love is kind. It does not envy,
it does not boast, it is not proud.
It does not dishonor others, it is not self-seeking, it is
not easily angered, it keeps no record of wrongs.
Love does not delight in evil but rejoices with the truth.
It always protects, always trusts, always hopes, always perseveres.
Love never fails."

Emotional Well-Being

1 Peter 5:7
"Cast all your anxiety on him because he cares for you.".

Inner Peace:

2 Thessalonians 3:16
"Now may the Lord of peace himself give you peace at all times in every way. The Lord be with all of you."

Gratitude:

Philippians 4:6
"Do not be anxious about anything, but in every situation, by prayer and petition, with thanksgiving, present your requests to God."

Courage & Strength:

Deuteronomy 31:6
"Be strong and courageous. Do not be afraid or terrified because of them, for the Lord your God goes with you; he will never leave you nor forsake you."

Boundaries:

Matthew 5:37
"All you need to say is simply 'Yes' or 'No'; anything
beyond this comes from the evil one."

I AM:

1 Corinthians 15:10
"But by the grace of God I am what I am, and his grace to
me was not without effect. No, I worked harder than all of
them, yet not I, but the grace of God that is with me."

Manifesting:

Matthew 6:33
"But seek first his kingdom and his righteousness,
and all these things will be given to you as well."

Mental Health Resources

National Domestic Violence Hotline Call 1-800-799-7233
Text: "BEGIN" to 88788
You can also chat with a representative at thehotline.org.

988 Suicide and Crisis Lifeline:
Call or text 988 for immediate assistance. You can
also chat with a representative at 988lifeline.org.

Self-harm Hotline:
Call (800) 366-8288
Visit www.helpguide.org

Veterans Crisis Line:
Call 1-800-273-TALK (8255) and press 1.
Crisis Text Line: Text the word "Home" to 741-741.

National Alliance on Mental Illness NAMI HelpLine:
Call 1-800-950-6264 or text NAMI to 741-741.

Substance Abuse and Mental Health Services
Administration's National Helpline:
Call 1-800-662-HELP (1-800-622-4357)

The Trevor Lifeline for LGBTQ Youth: Call 1-866-488-7386.

The Trans Lifeline: Call 1-877-565-8860.

······•))) ● (((•······

Single Parent Resources

The Life of a Single Mom
A national resource guide for single mothers and single fathers who need support in child care, finances, housing, health & wellness, job placements, Legal aid, mentoring services, transportation, education and so much more.
Website: Thelifeofasinglemom.com

Postpartum Support International (PSI)
Hotline Call or text 1-800-944-4773

National Maternal Mental Health Hotline:
Call 1-833-TLC-MAMA (1-833-852-6262).

1-800-4-A-Child (1-800-422-4453): A national hotline for immediate support and ideas

National Parent Helpline (1-855-427-2736): A helpline that offers emotional support and resources

1-800-CHILDREN website: A website that offers helpful resources and support

Parental Stress Line (1-800-632-8188): A 24/7 helpline that offers non-judgmental support for parents and caregivers

Printed in the United States
by Baker & Taylor Publisher Services

Printed in the United States
by Baker & Taylor Publisher Services